A Benjamin Blog
and his Inquisitive Dog
Investigation

Exploring
Mountains

Anita Ganeri

Heinemann
LIBRARY

Chicago, Illinois

To contact Capstone Global Library please
phone 800-747-4992, or visit our web site,
www.capstonepub.com

Edited by Dan Nunn, Rebecca Rissman, and Helen
Cox Cannons
Designed by Joanna Hinton-Malivoire
Original illustrations © Capstone Global Library Ltd
Illustrated by Sernur ISIK
Picture research by Mica Brancic
Production by Helen McCreath
Originated by Capstone Global Library Ltd

**Library of Congress Cataloging-in-Publication
Data**
Ganeri, Anita, 1961- author.
  Exploring mountains : a Benjamin Blog and his
inquisitive dog investigation / Anita Ganeri.
      pages cm.—(Exploring habitats, with Benjamin
Blog and his inquisitive dog)
   Includes bibliographical references and index.
  ISBN 978-1-4329-8776-3 (hb)—ISBN 978-1-4329-
8783-1 (pb) 1. Mountain ecology—Juvenile
literature. 2. Mountains—Juvenile literature. 3.
Mountain animals—Juvenile literature. I. Title.
QH541.5.M65G36 2014
551.43′2—dc23   2013017413

Acknowledgments
The author and publisher are grateful to the
following for permission to reproduce copyright
material: Alamy p. 15 (Mountain Light/© Galen
Rowell); Getty Images pp. 5 (Raja Islam), 8
(Photodisc/Stuart Dee), 10 (Aurora/Johnathan
Ampersand Esper), 22 (Nigel Pavitt), 25 (Time
Life Pictures/James Burke), 26 (AFP/Namgyal
Sherpa); Shutterstock pp. 6 (© mikenorton), 12 (©
pinggr), 14 (© Pablo H Caridad), 17 (© Mariusz
Niedzwiedzki), 18 (© Josh Schutz), 19 (© Ammit
Jack), 20 (© Krom1975), 21 (© Arsgera), 23 (© Ian
Woolcock), 24 (© Vixit), 27 (© Ian Woolcock), 29
top (© Roberto Cerruti), 29 bottom (© BG Smith);
SuperStock pp. 4 (National Geographic/Beth
Wald), 7 (Design Pics/Axiom Photographic), 9
(age fotostock), 11 (All Canada Photos/Claude
Robidoux), 13 (imagebroker.net), 16 (F1 ONLINE).

Cover photograph of a mountain landscape
reproduced with permission of Shutterstock
(© Pichugin Dmitry).

We would like to thank Michael Bright for his
invaluable help in the preparation of this book.

Every effort has been made to contact copyright
holders of any material reproduced in this book.
Any omissions will be rectified in subsequent
printings if notice is given to the publisher.

Some words are shown in bold, **like this**. You can find
out what they mean by looking in the glossary.

Contents

Welcome to the Mountains!

Hello! My name's Benjamin Blog and this is Barko Polo, my **inquisitive** dog. (He's named after the ancient ace explorer **Marco Polo**.) We have just returned from our latest adventure—exploring mountains around the world. We put this book together from some of the blog posts we wrote on the way.

BARKO'S BLOG-TASTIC MOUNTAIN FACTS

Mountains are roughly more than 3,333 feet (1,000 meters) high above their surrounding area. Some are much higher. A mountain called K2, between Pakistan and China, is 28,251 feet (8,611 meters) tall—lucky I'm not scared of heights!

Mountain Making

Posted by: Ben Blog | December 20 at 8:35 a.m.

The first stop on our trip was the Rocky Mountains in the United States. The Rockies are fold mountains. They were formed millions of years ago when two giant slabs of Earth's **crust** crashed into each other. This pushed the land in between upwards into giant folds.

BARKO'S BLOG-TASTIC MOUNTAIN FACTS

The Himalayas in Asia are the highest mountains on Earth. They were gradually formed after India crashed into the rest of Asia about 50 million years ago. What a sight!

Giant Blocks and Red-Hot Rocks

Posted by: Ben Blog | December 25 at 12:00 p.m.

From the Rockies, we headed across to Canada, where Barko took this photo of me in front of Mount Rundle. Mount Rundle is a block mountain. It was formed from a massive block of rock that got pushed up between two cracks in Earth's **crust**.

BARKO'S BLOG-TASTIC MOUNTAIN FACTS

Volcanoes happen when red-hot rock from deep underground comes up through cracks in Earth's crust. This is Cotopaxi in Ecuador. It hasn't **erupted** for 70 years, but I'm not going any closer, just in case!

Blowing Winds

Posted by: Ben Blog | January 14 at 3:16 p.m.

We are on the **summit** of Mount Kilimanjaro in Africa. Strong winds are blowing, and it's very cold. The higher up a mountain you go, the colder it gets. That's why there is ice and snow on the top of Kilimanjaro, even though it's near the steamy **equator**.

10

BARKO'S BLOG-TASTIC MOUNTAIN FACTS

A blizzard is a violent snowstorm that can blow up without warning. The wind blasts the snow into your face, so it's difficult to breathe or see anything. Who's there?

Knocked into Shape

We arrived in the Alps this morning and headed straight for the Matterhorn on the border between Italy and Switzerland. Here's one of the photos I took. Over millions of years, the wind, water, and changes in temperature have worn the mountain into its jagged shape.

BARKO'S BLOG-TASTIC MOUNTAIN FACTS

This flat-topped mountain is near Cape Town in South Africa. It is 3,559 feet (1,085 meters) high. The wind and rain have worn it into a shape like a table. Can you guess what it's called?

Flowing Ice, Falling Snow

Posted by: Ben Blog | March 17 at 4:00 p.m.

Glaciers are like gigantic rivers of ice that flow slowly down some mountain slopes. As they flow, they drag along rocks and boulders that scrape out U-shaped valleys in the mountainsides. This is the Perito Moreno Glacier in Argentina, and it's amazing.

BARKO'S BLOG-TASTIC MOUNTAIN FACTS

An **avalanche** is when thousands of tons of snow suddenly crash at high speed down a mountain. The snow buries everything in its way—trees, cars, houses, and people.

Living the High Life

Posted by: Ben Blog | April 2 at 9:18 a.m.

Animals need to be tough to live on a mountain. They have to cope with the cold, wind, snow, and steep slopes. I snapped this yak high up in the Himalayas, where it's bitterly cold. Luckily, yaks have very long, shaggy coats to keep them warm.

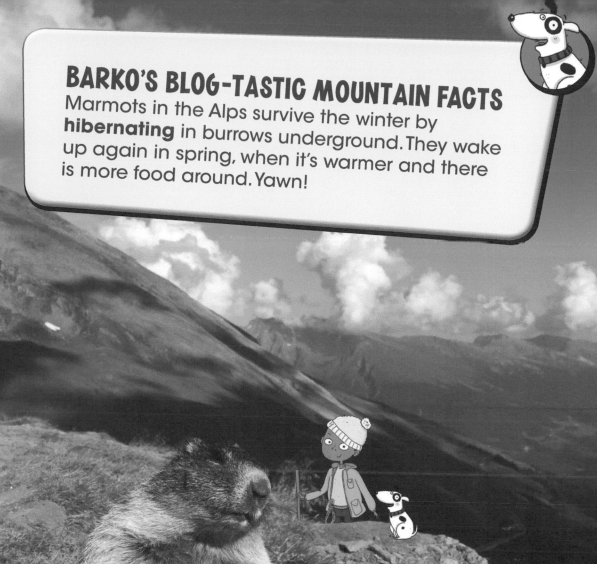

BARKO'S BLOG-TASTIC MOUNTAIN FACTS

Marmots in the Alps survive the winter by **hibernating** in burrows underground. They wake up again in spring, when it's warmer and there is more food around. Yawn!

We came across these mountain goats while we were scrambling about in the Rocky Mountains. They're great at climbing, even if the slopes are very steep. Their hooves have sharp edges for digging into cracks in the rocks and pads that stop them from slipping.

BARKO'S BLOG-TASTIC MOUNTAIN FACTS

Andean condors are massive birds that soar above the slopes of the Andes Mountains in South America. They have huge wings for gliding on gusts of wind.

Sprouting Slopes

Posted by: Ben Blog | July 10 at 1:00 p.m.

In summer, we headed back to the Alps to search for edelweiss. These tiny mountain plants have cleverly adapted to the cold and windy conditions. The first thing you notice about them is their furry leaves. These trap heat from the Sun and stop precious water from being lost.

BARKO'S BLOG-TASTIC MOUNTAIN FACTS

High up on a mountain, you can see a tree line, or a line where trees stop growing. Above the tree line, it's too cold and windy for trees to grow.

tree line

I took a photo of this amazing plant in the Aberdare Mountains of Kenya, in Africa. Most mountain plants grow low to the ground to stay out of the wind, but not this giant groundsel. Giant groundsels can reach 33 feet (10 meters) high. That's about six times as tall as me.

BARKO'S BLOG-TASTIC MOUNTAIN FACTS

The splashes of color on these rocks are tiny plant-like living things, called **lichen**. They make **acids** that **dissolve** the rocks. The lichen dig their hair-like roots into the cracks to fix themselves to the rocks.

High-Rise Everest

Posted by: Ben Blog | September 27 at 6:00 a.m.

Back in the Himalayas, we are getting ready to climb Mount Everest—the highlight of our trip. It won't be easy. Mount Everest is the highest mountain on Earth. It's 29,035 feet (8,850 meters) tall. It takes several days to climb from **base camp** to the **summit**. Wish us luck!

BARKO'S BLOG-TASTIC MOUNTAN FACTS

The first people to climb Mount Everest were Edmund Hillary from New Zealand and Tenzing Norgay from Nepal. They reached the summit on May 29, 1953.

Mountains of Trash

Posted by: Ben Blog | October 2 at 4:19 p.m.

We made it! Now it's back to **base camp** to pack up and pick up. Mountains are wonderful places for climbing, skiing, hiking, rafting, and **paragliding**. But people are leaving tons of trash behind, and it's making a terrible mess.

BARKO'S BLOG-TASTIC MOUNTAIN FACTS

Many mountain ranges have been made into national parks to protect them. You can see these amazing rocks in the Blue Mountains National Park in Australia. Legend says that they were once three sisters who were turned into stone.

Mighty Mountains Quiz

If you are planning your own mountain expedition, you need to be prepared. Find out how much you know about mighty mountains with our quick quiz.

1. What type of mountains are the Rockies?
a) fold
b) block
c) dome

2. What happens to the temperature the higher up you go?
a) it gets warmer
b) it gets colder
c) it stays the same

3. What is a **glacier**?
a) a sudden fall of snow
b) a type of mountain
c) a river of ice

4. How do yaks stay warm?
a) they **hibernate**
b) they have thick fur coats
c) they stay indoors

5. How do **lichens** break up rocks?
a) using acid
b) using hammers
c) using other rocks

6. Which is the world's highest mountain?
a) Everest
b) Kilimanjaro
c) K2

7. What is this?

8. What is this?

Glossary

acid liquid that breaks down rocks and other materials

avalanche sudden, massive fall of snow on a mountainside

base camp camp at the bottom of a mountain where climbers begin their climb

crust outer, rocky surface of Earth

dissolve turn something solid into liquid

equator imaginary line that runs around the middle of Earth

erupt when red-hot rock from underground comes up through cracks in Earth's crust

glacier huge river of ice that flows down a mountainside

hibernating sleeping during the winter when it is cold and there is little food about

inquisitive interested in learning about the world

lichen tiny plant-like living things that grow in crusty or bushy patches on trees and rocks

Marco Polo explorer who lived from about 1254 to 1324. He traveled from Italy to China.

paragliding sport where a person glides through the air, hanging from a wing-shaped parachute

summit top of a mountain

Find Out More

Books

Dickmann, Nancy. *Mount Everest* (Explorer Tales).
  Chicago: Raintree, 2013.

Ganeri, Anita. *Harsh Habitats.* Chicago:
  Raintree, 2013.

Green, Jen. *Mountains* (Geography Wise).
  New York: Rosen, 2011.

Underwood, Deborah. *Hiding in Mountains.*
  Chicago: Heinemann, 2011.

Web Sites

FactHound offers a safe, fun way to find Internet
sites related to this book. All of the sites on
FactHound have been researched by our staff.

Here's all you do:
Visit www.facthound.com
Type in this code: 9781432987763

Index